For Queen & Country

The Bands of Her Majesty's Royal Marines

A *year in pictures*

First published in the United Kingdom in July 2013
The Blue Band
Supply Officer Music Department
Headquarters Band Service Royal Marines
Eastney Block
HMS NELSON
Portsmouth
PO1 3HH

Copyright © The Blue Band 2013

Published by the Royal Marines Historical Society in association with 'The Blue Band'

Photography by Royal Naval photographers, the men and women of the Royal Marines Band Service and Mr Les Scriver MBE

The Blue Band is grateful to Henry Dallal for permission to use the photographs on pages 9, 10, 11

Text © John Ambler 2013

Printed and bound by PPG Print, Portsmouth

ISBN: Hardback 978-1-908123-07-7

Whilst every effort has been made to ensure the accuracy of the names and events mentioned within this book, the publisher and author cannot accept liability for any omissions or inaccuracies in its pages. The views expressed in the book are not necessarily those of the Ministry of Defence.

Contents

Foreword

Major General Ed Davis CBE

Commandant General Royal Marines & Commander Amphibious Forces

Throughout 2012 the Bands of Her Majesty's Royal Marines were at the forefront of National, and indeed global, events. These included celebrations for Her Majesty the Queen's Diamond Jubilee, Beating Retreat on Horse Guards Parade and the London 2012 Olympics alongside annual events such as the Mountbatten Festival of Music held in the Royal Albert Hall for the 40th year in succession. This pictorial book captures some of these events with images not generally seen by the public and many more including operational duty in Afghanistan.

The stellar performance of the Royal Marines Bands throughout the Queen's Diamond Jubilee celebrations in 2012 has ensured that the Royal Marines Band Service continues to be recognised across the World as the international benchmark for military musical excellence and innovation. These images illustrate why Military Bands remain an integral link between the Armed Forces and the general public, providing the glue that binds the 'fabric of the nation'. No major National event is complete without a Military Band presence; especially those with blue tunics, white helmets and drums beating.

Manifestly, the Royal Marines Band Service remains a peerless Military Band. The professionalism, innovation and precision with which the Bands carry out their duties remains the standard to which most other Military Bands can only aspire. It is testament to their brilliance that they make us all immensely proud at each and every performance.

Introduction
Lieutenant Colonel NJ Grace OBE RM
Principal Director of Music Royal Marines & Commandant Royal Marines School of Music

I firmly believe that the Royal Marines Band Service provides the Naval Service, Defence and the State with the visible manifestation of musical and ceremonial excellence that underpins the fabric of the nation, Service ethos and national core values. Without doubt, 2012 was a uniquely historic year for the whole Nation where the Bands of Her Majesty's Royal Marines would participate and form an integral part in many of the major events.

As Principal Director of Music, Royal Marines, it has been my honour to lead the men and women of the Royal Marines Band Service preceding, during and since the events of 2012 in supporting the Naval Service, Defence and especially Her Majesty the Queen at the various National and State Ceremonial occasions.

Throughout this book you will see the wide variety of events, both musical and operational, that our Royal Marines Bands have been involved in. There is obviously a focus upon several key moments including the Queen's Diamond Jubilee Celebrations, the Olympics and Paralympic Games, the Mountbatten Festival of Music, Massed Bands Beating Retreat and Ceremonial Sunset on Horse Guards Parade and a number of other significant engagements and activities both at home and abroad.

None of this could be achieved without the highly focused and effective music training at the Royal Marines School of Music. Training is both comprehensive and demanding in equal measure and vital in developing the necessary skills to enable the Royal Marines Band Service to deliver specialist musical and military support of the highest professional standards that the Nation expects.

Allied to the musical commitments of Royal Marine Bands, there was the continued important Operational Role and deployments on operations to Afghanistan. The adaptability and versatility of the men and women in this dual role of providing specific military support whilst at the same time providing musical entertainment has had a significantly positive effect on the morale of deployed troops. Bringing operational military music to the front-line should never be underestimated, and musicians and buglers of the Royal Marines continue to deliver this at every opportunity.

A book such as this requires a tremendous amount of work and contributions from a whole range of people. I would particularly like to acknowledge the special contributions made by: WO1 Tom Hodge MBE, Mr John Ambler, WO1 Dean Waller, BdCSgt Paul Meacham, Mr Les Scriver MBE, Mr Henry Dallal (pictures pages 9 – 11), Major Jon Ridley, Dr Liz LeGrove, Colonel Brian Carter OBE, various Royal Navy photographers, serving members of the Royal Marines Band Service who have provided material used in the book and the Royal Navy and Royal Marines Charities.

This book is by no means meant as a comprehensive record of the thousand-plus engagements undertaken by all bands, but perhaps just a pictorial snapshot showing the variety of these engagements and commitments in which the Bands of Her Majesty's Royal Marines have been involved supporting our 'Queen and Country' in 2012.

The Queen's Diamond Jubilee

On the 12th February 1952, Princess Elizabeth acceded to the throne as Queen Elizabeth II. A few days later the funeral of her father, King George VI, took place. The Band of the Plymouth Group, Royal Marines, augmented by musicians from the Royal Marines School of Music and under the command of Captain R H Stoner, led the officers and men of the Royal Navy, including the seamen drawing the gun-carriage that bore the coffin, and the Royal Marines. The Coronation of Queen Elizabeth II took place on the 2nd June 1953. Royal Navy and Royal Marine processional contingents were led by the Band of Portsmouth Group under Captain K A McLean. Also providing music in the parade were the bands of Plymouth Group and the Royal Marines School of Music. Paraded with the Royal Marine battalion in Trafalgar Square were the massed bands of Commander-in-Chief, Portsmouth, and HMS *Excellent*. Major F V Dunn was the Admiralty representative on the committee co-ordinating the music played by military bands. In 2012, following sixty years service to Her Majesty, the Royal Marines Band Service was placed at the forefront of events that marked the Diamond Jubilee of Queen Elizabeth II.

Armed Forces Parade and Muster

This tribute consisted of a parade through the Windsor Castle Quadrangle and a muster and Drumhead Service in Windsor Great Park Arena. The Royal Marines Band Service provided a band with the tri-service Guard of Honour in the quadrangle, two bands leading the parade, musicians in the tri-service stage band and ensembles playing in the Royal Marquee and the Royal Navy Marquee. As Britain's senior military musician the Principal Director of Music, Royal Marines, was responsible for all aspects of musical support.

"As Chief of the Defence Staff I could not be more pleased and confident in the leading role you, and Corps' musicians, will be playing."

General Sir David Richards GCB CBE DSO ADC Gen
Chief of Defence Staff

Windsor Pageant

A complex stage and arena show featuring international acts and based upon the Queen's travels and her love of horses. The Royal Marines Band Service provided the stage band of fifty musicians and a fourteen-piece fanfare team. This massed band, plus a large choir and musicians from London orchestras, were all conducted by the Principal Director of Music, Royal Marines. The Windsor Pageant was broadcast on ITV as part of the main Diamond Jubilee weekend celebrations.

"Their contribution helped turn a dream into reality and a concept into a stunning live show."

Simon Brookes-Ward LVO OBE TD
Director & Producer

River Thames Pageant

Despite the weather the River Pageant went ahead. The Royal Marines Band Plymouth with the Principal Director of Music and the Corps Drum Major were on board the *Vallula*. Six buglers with herald trumpets were aboard the *Connaught*. Two fanfares were played before the *Connaught* sailed, another as the Queen's barge joined the flotilla and then each time the vessel passed below a bridge. The band aboard *Vallula* played music and marches associated with sailing and the sea.

"In all my years service that was the best gig I have ever done"

Sergeant Bugler Sean Donaghue RM

The early morning sound check

Saluting Her Majesty The Queen who was aboard *Spirit of Chartwell*

Regular Major Events

Within any diary or programme there will always be a number of important regular events that occur annually or at lesser or greater intervals. Their recurrence means they are important; they are meaningful, they are traditional. Three major events of this type occurred in the Royal Marines Band Service calendar for 2012. Each was very different from the others. The Mountbatten Festival of Music featuring the massed bands on stage at the Royal Albert Hall has been an annual occurrence since 1973. The Ceremony of Beating Retreat on Horse Guards Parade is a display of precision drill based upon the early military duties of Beating Retreat and Sunset. Their origins can be traced back to the 17th century, possibly earlier. The third, *Eternal Voices*, a concert of Remembrance to be performed in our great cathedrals, was born out of recent events in Iraq and Afghanistan and 2012 witnessed its third annual performance. In addition to these three major events, illustrated in the next few pages, there are many others that occur time after time for the individual Royal Marines Bands. Many are in support of Service, and other, Charities or ex-Service organisations.

Mountbatten Festival of Music

This annual series of concerts at the Royal Albert Hall, performed by 'The Massed Bands of Her Majesty's Royal Marines', is now believed to be the longest running, and largest, of its kind in the world. Additionally, members of the Royal Marines Band Service take responsibility for all creative, planning, technical and performance aspects and frequently the musical programme is almost entirely composed or arranged by past or serving members. In 2012 the production of a DVD recording was an additional feature.

First rehearsal in Portsmouth Guildhall

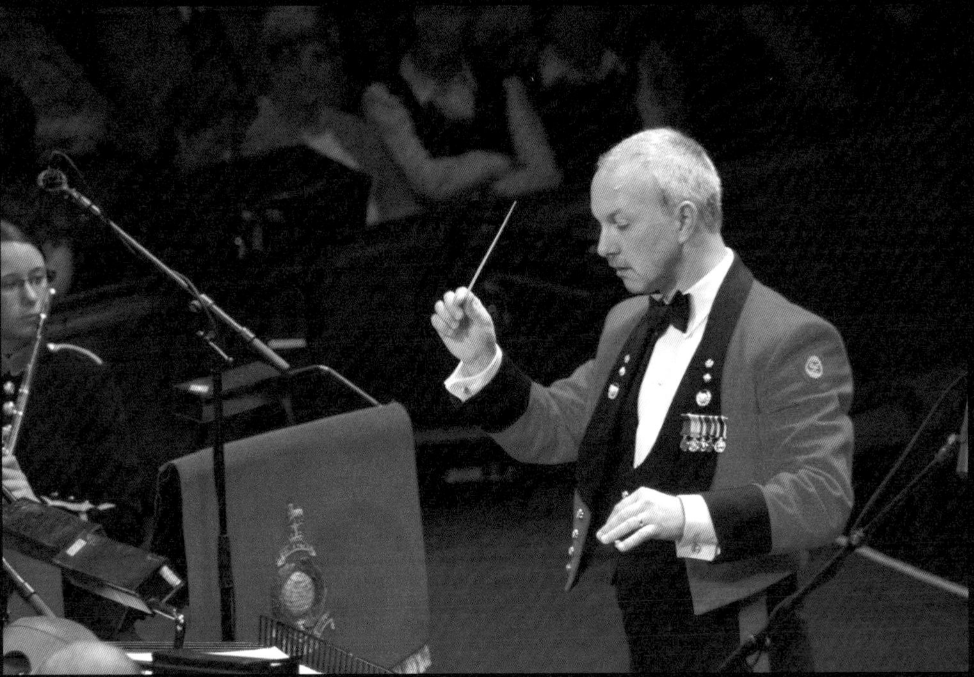

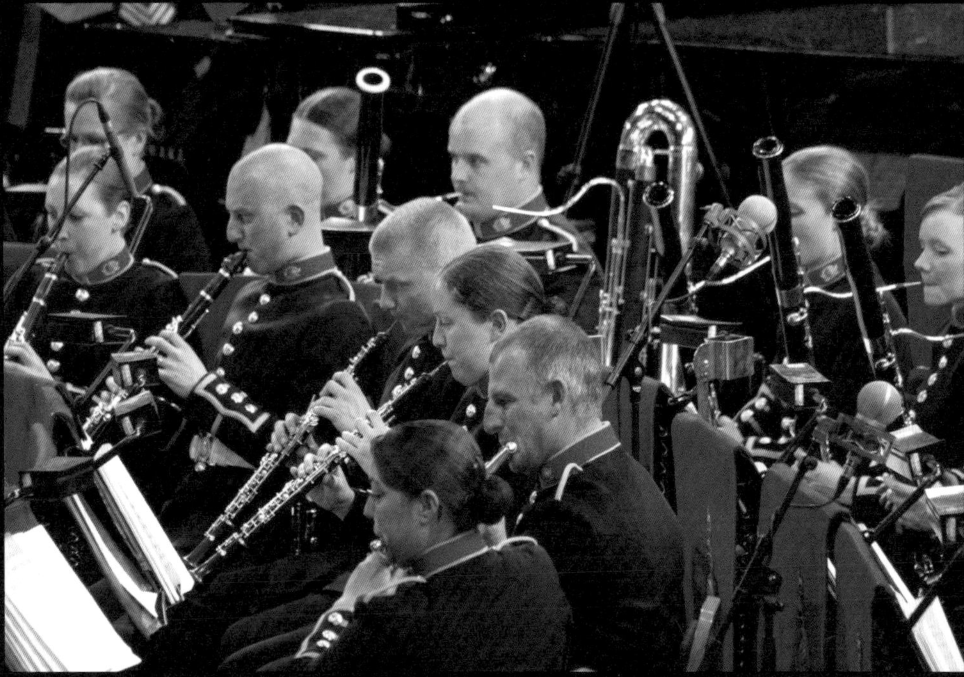

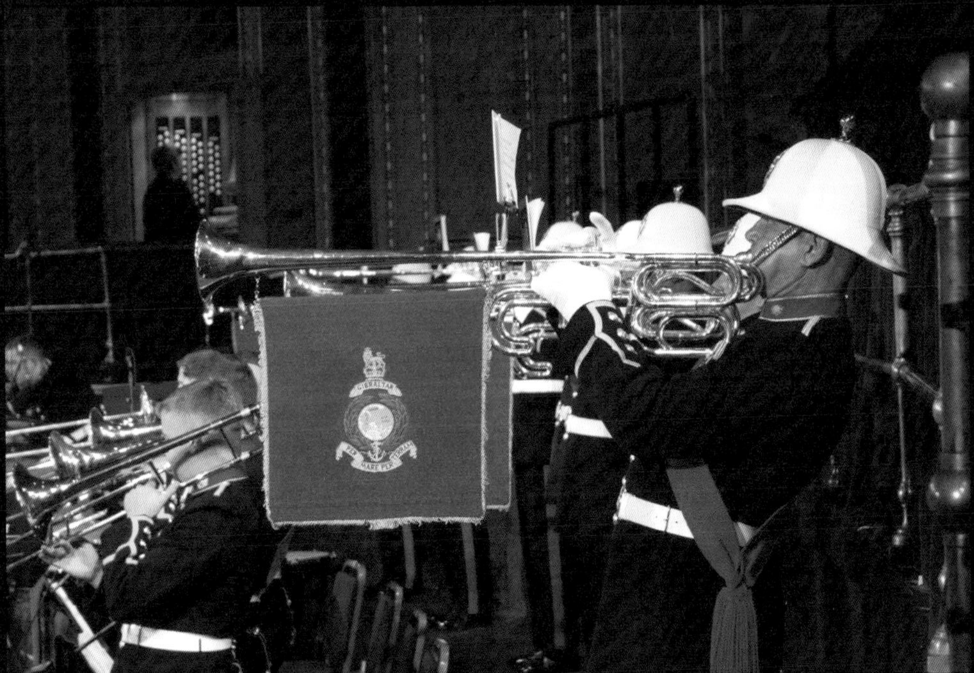

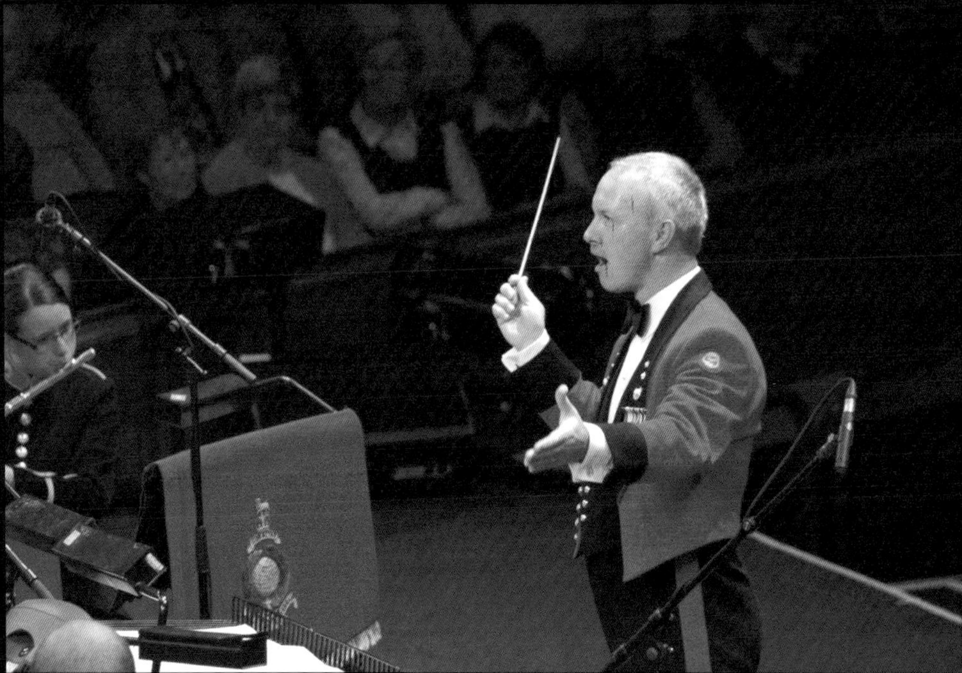

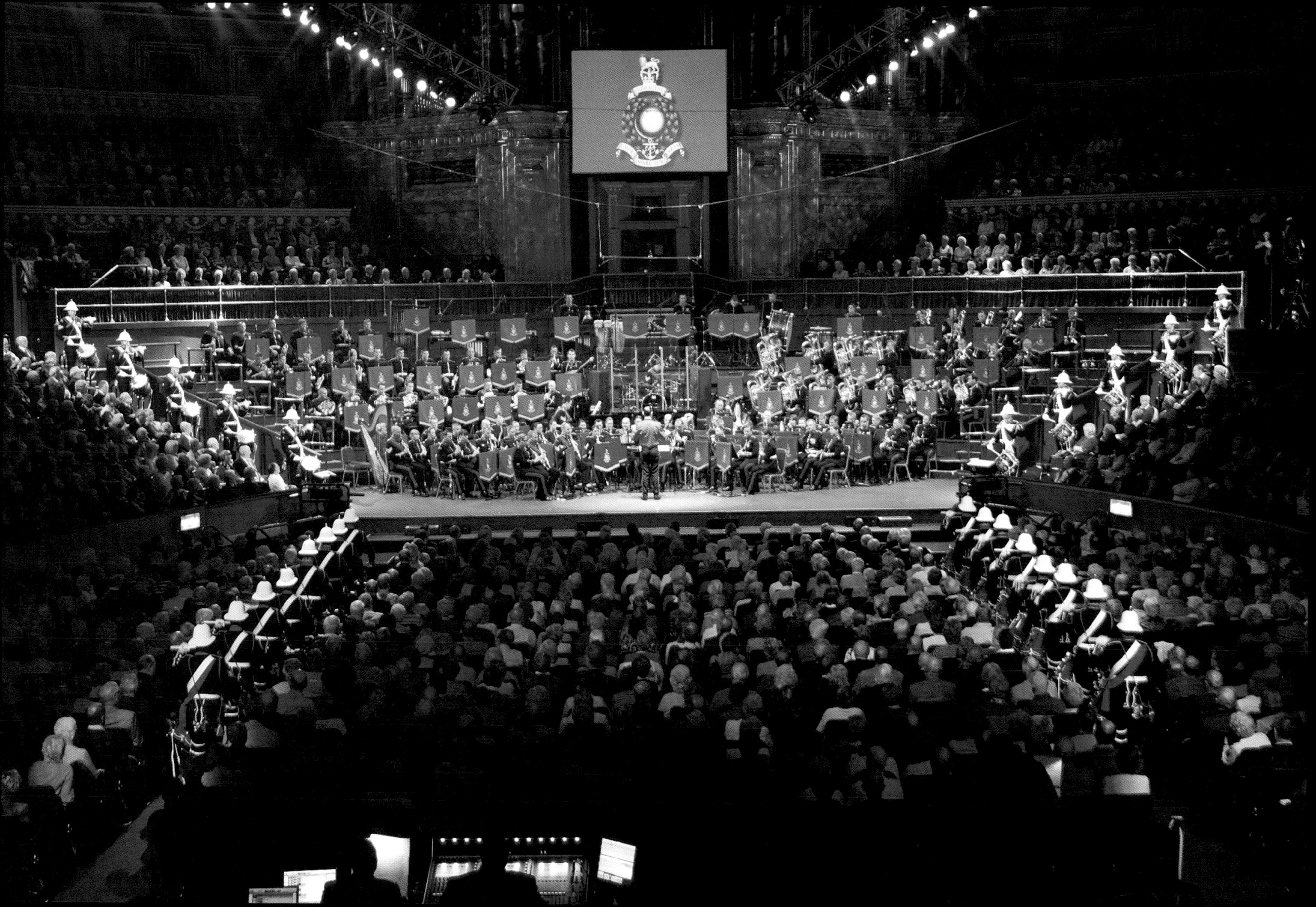

The Ceremony of Beating Retreat

At regular intervals the Massed Bands of the Royal Marines march on to Horse Guards Parade in London to perform a musical marching display to celebrate the birthday of His Royal Highness Prince Philip, The Duke of Edinburgh and Captain General, Royal Marines. This display is based upon the ceremonies of Beating Retreat and Sunset. Traditionally, these were carried out by drummers but, during the twentieth century, the music of the bands was added. Unfortunately, because of illness, His Royal Highness was unable to attend on this occasion.

Massed Bands musical rehearsal in Portsmouth Bandroom

Rehearsals at HMS *Excellent*, Whale Island

Rehearsals on Horse Guards Parade

"There could not have been a more appropriate conclusion to this historic and intense period of events than the flawless performance produced by the Massed Bands of Her Majesty's Royal Marines on Horse Guards Parade."

Lieutenant Colonel Nick Grace OBE RM
Principal Director of Music Royal Marines &
Commandant Royal Marines School of Music

"*I do like it when Massed Bands start parading down Birdcage Walk on our way towards Horse Guards, and the whole of our Nation's Capital knows we are here...*"

Band Colour Sergeant Paul Bateman RM

Pictured left - The guest of honour, General JF Amos USMC,
Commandant of the United States Marine Corps, with
Major General EGM Davis CBE, Commandant General Royal Marines

"The quality of music and skill of the Massed Bands of Her Majesty's Royal Marines was world class and vivid testament to the brilliance of our devoted and highly talented musicians..."

Major General Ed Davis CBE
Commandant General Royal Marines

The Massed Bands of Her Majesty's Royal Marines march along The Mall towards Buckingham Palace

Eternal Voices Concert

This 'Concert of Remembrance', was performed in Chichester Cathedral by the Royal Marines Band Portsmouth and three local choirs: the Otter Consort, the Chichester Chorale and the University Chamber Choir. The central piece of music, *Eternal Voices*, features a soprano and boy treble as the wife and son of a fallen Royal Marine. A narrator provides news bulletins between the five movements of this thirty-minute work. Both concert and recording raise money for the Royal Marines Charitable Trust Fund.

The Operational Role

Preparations for the events of 2012 were influenced by Royal Marines Band Service operational duties of 2011. These are illustrated in the following pages. Royal Marines buglers have had a continuous dual role since 1664 when, as drummers, they were raised with the Marines. The musician's military, or secondary, role began at the beginning of the First World War when Royal Marine Bands first became part of the ship's gunnery control organisation. Many musicians and buglers were killed during the two World Wars. Since 1982 when two bands served with the Task Force in the Falklands, the military role has become more formalised, more integrated and more frequent. Musicians and buglers have carried out operational duties in Iraq (1991), Kosovo (2000), Iraq (2003), Cyprus (2007) and Afghanistan during 2007, 2008-2009, 2010 and 2011. Buglers have, in addition, served with all Commando Unit deployments to Afghanistan. These recent operational deployments dictate that the Royal Marines Band Service constantly reviews its military capability and operational roles. The period of recruit military training has been extended and is now carried out at the Commando Training Centre, Royal Marines.

Afghanistan - Operation Herrick 14

The United Kingdom's Joint Force Medical Group included men and women of the Royal Marines Band Service, principally employed as ambulance drivers and signallers. Ambulance Response Troop transported over 2000 casualties of all nationalities, receiving the 2011 Ambulance Society Institute Military Award. A Band Service officer served as Regimental Adjutant whilst musicians and buglers provided 'top cover' and drove battlefield ambulances on Combat Logistic Patrols. A Senior NCO was awarded the Queen's Commendation for Valuable Service. Apart from the audiences, all personnel seen in the images in this chapter are Royal Marines Band Service personnel.

Preparing a battlefield ambulance before a patrol

Driver and 'Top Cover' - Battlefield ambulance during a Combat Logistics Patrol

Troop entertainment in Camp Bastion

The Royal Marines Band Commando Training Centre at the medals award ceremony

Afghanistan Showband

Unlike other Royal Marines Bands deployed to Afghanistan, the purpose of this Showband was to take music and instruments appropriate to the age and musical interest of the coalition troops serving in the operational theatre. This entertainment was made available in a variety of environments ranging from Camp Bastion Hospital to Patrol Base 2 at Nahr-e Saraj and including Camp Price, Camp Souter, Kandahar, Kabul and Lashkar Gah. Weapons were carried at all times and training was geared to ensuring the musicians were as self-reliant, in terms of movement and security, as possible. This was bringing operational military music directly to the frontline.

Zeroing weapons - Camp Bastion ranges

The Rock Band prepare to entertain 1st Bn The Rifles at Patrol Base 2 near Nahr-e Saraj

Adaptability and teamwork in Kandahar!

Concert at Kabul International Airport

Rock Band concert at the Kandahar NAAFI

DEAL
BLOCK

The Royal Marines School of Music

The head of the Royal Marines Band Service is the Principal Director of Music, Royal Marines, with the rank of Lieutenant Colonel. He is also Commandant of the Royal Marines School of Music. His responsibilities include the provision of musical and operational support to the Naval Service. Unlike many organisations, any recruit musician can aspire to become Principal Director of Music. There is no Direct Officer Entrant scheme; everyone starts as a musician or as a bugler. The Royal Marines Band Service is a fully integrated, homogeneous organisation. Virtually self-supporting, it encourages development into various areas of experience. It fosters initiative, acceptance of responsibility and ambition to learn and to progress.

Royal Marines School of Music Military Training

This physically and mentally demanding training is undertaken at The Commando Training Centre Royal Marines by all Royal Marines School of Music recruits. The fifteen week course is similar to the first phase of Royal Marines Commando training. Of the twenty-three members of Troop 1/12, twenty-two successfully completed the training; a testament to the selection process, the Royal Marines Band Service Training Team and to their own ability and determination. Following their Passing Out Parade the recruits commence their musical training.

Introduction to fitness training - HMS *Nelson* gym

In the field - preparing for kit inspection

The first experience of personal protection breathing equipment

The Royal Marines Band Service member of the Royal Marines Commando Military Training Team inspects parts of a recruit's rifle.

Still smiling!

Troop 1/12 Military Training Inspection, Display and Passing Out Parade at the Commando Training Centre Royal Marines

Musical Training at the Royal Marines School of Music

Including New Entry Military Training, musicians and buglers spend up to three years under training. All musicians have to play an orchestral and a wind band instrument whilst buglers are trained on military side drum, the bugle and the herald trumpet. Parade work requires a sound knowledge of band drill to be acquired by all. As they pass through the latter stages of their training, musicians and buglers will undertake a number of training engagements. These culminate in the Open Day Concert in Portsmouth Guildhall and the Ceremony of Beating Retreat in the Guildhall Square.

Music and band drill, the fundamentals of ceremonial, are instilled into the trainees

Marching displays in Portsmouth present opportunities
for performing for, and meeting, the public

"One of the proudest moments in my Service career as a Bandmaster was conducting the The Royal Marines School of Music Ceremonial Marching Band at the Guildhall Square in Portsmouth. The professionalism and enthusiasm of our young trainee Musicians and Buglers bodes well for the future"

Warrant Officer Class 1 Bandmaster Dean Waller RM
Bandmaster Training

The Band of the Royal Marines School of Music playing at an open-air concert at the Royal Marines Museum

Royal Marines School of Music Open Day
& Passing Out Parade

Parents, as well as other family and friends, have the opportunity to view the facilities used by their sons and daughters during their training at the Royal Marines School of Music. This is followed by an awards ceremony and then a Passing Out Parade for those 'Passing for Duty' before joining their allocated bands. On this occasion Vice-Admiral Sir Charles Montgomery KBE ADC, Second Sea Lord, took the salute.

The Second Sea Lord takes the salute as troop 1/09 pass for duty

Higher Training Department

The most advanced course delivered by the Royal Marines School of Music's Higher Training Department is the Bandmasters' Course. This one-year course focuses on conducting, composing and arranging. Upon successful completion the student is musically qualified for the rank of Warrant Officer Bandmaster. An important part of the course is the series of public concerts at which students conduct the full orchestra, the wind band and other ensembles.

A student bandmaster rehearses the orchestra under the attentive eyes of the senior staff of the Higher Training Department

"to be given the opportunity to guide the future has been an honour and a privilege..."

Warrant Officer Class 2 Bandmaster Ashley Williams RM
Chief Instructor Higher Training

Pictured right - The Orchestra of the Royal Marines Band Portsmouth and Collingwood at St Mary's Church, Portsmouth

Command Training

The joint Junior and Senior Command Course begins with Basic Fitness and Combat Fitness Tests. Revision of map reading, navigation, patrolling and section attack techniques then precede an exercise in Hampshire. The Commando Training Centre is attended for training in leadership, radio, casualty evacuation, burial of the dead and the manning of Vehicle Check Points. A further exercise, in Wales, tests the candidates' aptitude for command during a military action. Event management and similar administrative and organisational training is followed by the tough and competitive Endurance Course, and the Stretcher Carry.

2012 Olympics

Prior to 2012, the last time that Great Britain hosted the Olympic Games was in 1948 at a time of great austerity. The Olympic flame was brought from Greece to Wembley Stadium. One of the torch bearers, during its journey across Greece itself, was Musician F Greenwood of HMS *Phoebe's* Royal Marine Band, one of two men selected from the Royal Navy's Mediterranean Fleet. Olympic sailing events were held off Torquay and, due to the distance from London, Torquay had its own Opening and Closing Ceremonies including an Olympic Flame brought from Wembley Stadium by runners. Sixty-four years later the Royal Marines Band Service was not only called upon for musical support at the nautical events but also at a range of other events and venues during both the Olympics and the Paralympics of 2012.

The Olympic Flame

The Royal Marines Band Commando Training Centre played a significant role at Royal Naval Air Station *Culdrose* when the Olympic flame arrived in Great Britain. The Princess Royal and other guests watched as, to the sound of the fanfare team, the cauldron was lit by David Beckham. The finale was the Ceremony of Beating Retreat. This was the beginning of the Olympic flame's journey around Britain, during which it passed through Portsmouth, where the Corps of Drums of the Royal Marines Band Portsmouth provided the ceremonial aspect of the occasion.

A fanfare is sounded as David Beckham lights the first British torch from the Olympic flame

"Being a part of the Olympics as a whole was fantastic but the highlight for me was performing a fanfare as the Olympic Torch came into the Historic Dockyard..."

Corporal Bugler S Warmington RM

Olympic Events

The Royal Marines Band Collingwood supported the Olympic Rowing events at Eton Dorney, providing marching displays and performing the Ceremony of Beating Retreat. HMS *Bulwark* provided the HQ and logistic base for Royal Marines Units providing security for the sailing events at Weymouth. The ship hosted the Great Britain Sailing Team and, as part of the event, they were entertained by a Royal Marines Big Band. The Portsmouth Band supported Beach Volleyball on Horse Guards Parade, and was on the Mall for the Marathon.

London Ceremonial

For three weeks, the Royal Marines Band Portsmouth provided music to welcome visitors to the Olympic Park. They also provided music at a parade to thank the Armed Services for their contribution to the events. Following the success of the British Olympians and Paralympians, a celebratory parade through London took place. The route was from Mansion House to the Queen Victoria Memorial outside Buckingham Palace. Musical support for the emotive day was provided by the Royal Marines Band Collingwood.

The Royal Marines National Memorial on the Mall is saluted as the Royal Marines Band Collingwood march past

Other Musical Events

2012 has not just been a year of special events for the Royal Marines Band Service. Every year requests for their appearance at parades, for ceremonial and in concert are far greater than can be accommodated; priorities have to be assessed and decisions taken. For this special year demands were greater and expectations higher; so decisions were even harder. Television shows, film premieres, concerts, tattoos, visits by VIPs, supporting the Royal Navy and the Royal Marines as well as work for a range of Service Charities throughout the United Kingdom placed a heavy work-load upon the bands. In addition, important visits overseas, promoting the British image and working with the Armed Forces of allies around the world, continued and is a demanding role. Importantly, and increasingly in the public heart and mind, there is Remembrance.

British Musical Events

Whilst concerts and Beating Retreat ceremonies provide regular work for the bands, the spectrum of music provision has increased in recent years. 2012, possibly because of the Diamond Jubilee and Olympic events, was particularly varied. Appearances on television shows such as *'League of their Own'* and *'Strictly Come Dancing'*, as well as the World Premiere of James Bond's *'Skyfall'*, rubbed shoulders with regular events such as *'Music of the Night'*, and leading the multi-national performers in the *'Royal Edinburgh Military Tattoo'*

'Music of the Night' – the tenth, and final, annual joint concert by the Royal Marines Band Plymouth and the Royal Artillery Band at the Royal Citadel, Plymouth

The British Formula One Grand Prix, Silverstone

The Band of The Commando Training Centre with Eddie Jordan OBE, former racing driver, tv personality and also a keen drummer

At the *Royal Edinburgh Military Tattoo* the Tri-Service massed bands were joined by international performers

The Royal Marines Band Collingwood recording music for *'Strictly Come Dancing'* at the BBC Maida Vale Studios, London

The Prime Minister inspects the Royal Marines Band Plymouth at the Britannia Royal Naval College, Dartmouth Passing Out Parade

The world premiere of the James Bond film *'Skyfall'* was preceded by a Corps of Drums
marching display outside the Royal Albert Hall and a band display on stage

HMS *Diamond* returned to Portsmouth at the end of Diamond Jubilee year to be welcomed by the sight and sound of the Royal Marines Band Portsmouth

Rehearsal and preparation - the key to successful performance

A string quartet in the Admiral's Cabin aboard HMS *Victory*, Portsmouth

Overseas Tours and Events

A varied range of events took place around the world during 2012. In size they ranged from events such as the Brass Quintet provided for the Barakura English Garden Festival and Fashion Show in Japan, to the Tattoos held in Trinidad and Tobago and, later, Jamaica. Two bands were invited, at different times, to visit Baltimore and Washington in the United States of America. It is equally important not to forget the Volunteer Band Instructors provided by the Royal Marines Band Service; these men and women also get the opportunity to serve at sea and abroad.

The Ceremony of Beating Retreat performed for the First Sea Lord by the Royal Marines Band Commando Training Centre on RFA *Argus*, Baltimore, Maryland

The Royal Marines Band Plymouth led the celebrations for the 50th Anniversary of Trinidad and Tobago at Port of Spain

"Music is an enabler that can be utilised to influence, build rapport beyond language and cultural barriers, and assist in building relationships with foreign governments"

Warrant Officer Class 1 Bandmaster Martin Grace RM
Bandmaster RM Band Portsmouth

The United States Naval Academy Band at Annapolis hosted the Royal Marines Band Scotland in Washington DC during the events marking the War of 1812, the United States' "second war of independence"

For the eleventh consecutive year a brass quintet entertained at the Barakura English Garden Festival and Fashion Show, Japan

Somewhere at Sea! The Royal Marines Volunteer Band Instructor aboard HMS *Illustrious* rehearsing his band in a machinery space and working as Ship's Postman

Remembrance

Although chiefly associated with the November Ceremonies, the participation of the Royal Marines Band Service in Remembrance is far greater than this. Armed Forces Day at various locations; the annual concert on the Deal Memorial Bandstand, where the Royal Marines musicians killed and injured in 1989 are remembered, and the Royal Marines Band Service Memorial Weekend in October are especially meaningful to past and present members of the Royal Marines Band Service. In addition there are the preparations for, and participation in, the National Commemorations in November.

Armed Forces Day,
Caernarfon

Deal Memorial Bandstand Concert

The audience at the Royal Marines Band Service Reunion appreciate the performance by the Band of the Royal Marines School of Music

The Royal Marines Band Service

MEMORIAL DAY SERVICE

Sunday 14 October 2012

(1100am for 1130am)

*The Cathedral Church of S*t* Thomas of Canterbury*
Portsmouth

BEFORE THE SERVICE

Orchestra	**La Calinda**	Delius (1862-1934)
	Clair de Lune	Debussy (1862-1918)
	Meditation from 'Thaïs'	Massenet (1842-1912)
	Scènes Pittoresque (Movements 1, 2 & 3)	Massenet (1842-1912)

Music performed by
The Orchestra of the
Bands of Her Majesty's Royal Marines
Portsmouth (Royal Band) and Collingwood
Conducted by
Lieutenant Colonel NJ Grace Royal Marines,
Principal Director of Music Royal Marines

and

Portsmouth Cathedral Choir
and Cathedral Youth Choir
Conducted by
Dr David JC Price HonDMus GMus(TCL) HonFASC

Organist
Oliver Hancock

"And we come to celebrate and to remember the people who create and bring their music, not just to churches and concert halls but to the places where humanity struggles in the darkest sense. The places of fear and conflict, the place of war"

Revd Mike Meachin BTh RN
CSFC Chaplain
Chaplaincy Team Leader HMS Collingwood

The 'Memorial Trumpets of the Royal Naval School of Music', later titled 'The Memorial Silver Trumpets of the Royal Marines School of Music' - the official War Memorial for the Second World War when 225 men of the Royal Marine Bands were killed.

A brass ensemble, with two buglers, aboard HMS *Victory*, Portsmouth, on Trafalgar Day

Preparing for the London November ceremonies; buglers assist rehearsal of the Royal Navy street-lining party on Whale Island, Portsmouth

"The piece was delivered with consummate style and precision and was without doubt the best I have seen at this event; the spontaneous reaction of the audience on completion spoke volumes for the Band's professionalism."

Admiral Sir Mark Stanhope GCB OBE ADC
The First Sea Lord

The Royal Marines Band Collingwood, wearing the distinctive band capes, play at the Royal Navy's principal commemorative event for Remembrance Sunday; Portsmouth Guildhall Square

Supply & Support

The ability of the Royal Marines Band Service to be efficient and cost-effective whilst maintaining its significant reputation is not solely due to musicianship. The cohesive organisation includes teams and individuals, either from the musical ranks or civilians, who are able to provide specialist skills or knowledge. A team of highly-skilled civilian craftsmen are employed in the Musical Instrument Workshop maintaining and repairing orchestral and wind band instruments in a manner that could not be provided elsewhere. Musicians and buglers have expanded their musical expertise into areas such as sound engineering and recording, stage management and lighting, in-house publishing and also take responsibility for the highly regarded Central Music Library. In the next few pages some of these men and women will be seen using their skills in support of the needs of the Royal Marines Band Service.

"Quality Sound reinforcement is vital to the success of any production. I have been fortunate to learn from some of the industry's finest; this combined with 'military based' production planning allows one to sit and mix what can only be described as 'World Class' musical events..."

Band Colour Sergeant A Deacon RM
RM Band Service Recording/Production SNCO

The Recording and Production Team Manager, a Senior NCO
qualified in audio engineering, working in the Recording Studio

The clean, uncluttered working environment necessary for the Woodwind…

Percussion…

Stringed…

and Brass Instrument specialists

"The Central Music Library is a treasure trove of historic records of original works hand written by composers such as Woodfield, Goodwin and Dunn. We support many musical organisations from the tri-service Military Bands to the civilian musical ensembles throughout the country"

Band Sergeant D Johnson RM
Royal Marines Band Service Central Music Library

Sport

This section provides an insight into the essential, although perhaps not realised, exploits of the very fit musicians and buglers of the Royal Marines Band Service. Many make time to represent the Royal Navy, the Royal Marines, or just themselves, in competitive sports. In addition to the sports illustrated in the following pages, the men and women of the Royal Marines Band Service have successfully competed, often at a senior level, in sports such as hockey, triathlon – where a musician took gold in the Royal Marines Open – cricket, motor rallying, cycling and mountaineering. Sports are also amongst the diverse range of activities undertaken as Adventure Training, officially defined as "To develop individual courage, leadership skills and teamwork through controlled exposure to risk in a challenging outdoor environment…" Such challenging activities range from walking and climbing on Dartmoor to parachuting, gliding, sailing and caving.

A musician, recently introduced to the Biathlon competition, is now part of the Royal Navy/Royal Marines Biathlon Team

Alpine Winter Sports Championships; this musician has, for a number of years, successfully competed in many events as a member of the Royal Navy Team

A number of musicians and buglers compete for the Royal Navy and the Royal Marines Equestrian Teams

Band football teams regularly take part in Royal Marines and Royal Marines Band Service competitions. Many athletes take part in Charity events - four completed the Great South Run - whilst others prefer the climbs, the mud and the tough conditions of the eleven mile, off-road, 'Hell Run'

The Royal Marines Band Service 2012

The Bands of Her Majesty's Royal Marines undertook one thousand five hundred and ninety-one engagements during the year of 2012

Subscribers

John Ambler
Paul Bateman, Ottawa, Canada
Maj J Burcham RM, Director of Music (Training)
Ray Collins, Croydon, Surrey
Terry Crook, Gidea Park, Romford
Capt P J Curtis MBE RM, Director of Music RM Band Portsmouth
Carol Davies
Jim Davies, Pyrford
Kathleen Davies
Major A J Donald RM
Bob Farrow, Calmore, Hants
Mark Gilbertson, Macclesfield, Cheshire
WO1 Bandmaster Martin Grace RM, Bandmaster RM Band Portsmouth
Lt Col N J Grace OBE RM, Principal Director of Music Royal Marines
Capt Andy Gregory RM, Director of Music RM Band Scotland
Bd CSgt Sam Hairsine RM, HMS Heron
Terry Hissey
WO1 Bandmaster Tom Hodge MBE RM
Musician 'Minty' Lambert
Corps Bug Maj Tommy Lawton MSM
B S Libby, Torpoint
Philip Marrow, Chorley, Lancashire

Bd CSgt Paul Meacham RM
Sue and Stephen Merrell
Kerrie and Lizzie Merrell-Silk
Alan Purdie, Hampton, Middlesex
Maj Jon Ridley RM
G Roper, Australia
Bd Cpl Eva Rose RM, Brighton
Jonathan Saunders, Wigmore, Kent
Sheila Ann Scala
Les Scriver MBE, Photographer
Mike Shelvey, Gravesend, Kent
Jan and Lee Silk
Mr Richard D Stone, Shanklin, IoW
Stephen Summerfield, Burgess Hill
Miss J M Tearle, Farnborough
Sgt Bugler Andy Travis
WO1 Bandmaster Dean Waller RM, Supply Officer (Music)
Bd Cpl Claire Walsh RM
Cpl Bugler 'Warmy' Warmington RM
May Welch, St Albans
Peter Wiseman, Beckenham, Kent
Adam Wilson